# Consequence of Dream

# Consequence of Dream

## Kevin Finn

Six Gallery Press

6GP115

ISBN 978-1-989305-17-1


Six Gallery Press
P.O. Box 90145
Pittsburgh, PA 15224
www.sixgallerypress.com

*for EVR*

*and*

*to Lucy*

# Table of Contents

SURFACE HEAT

GATHERED TRIUNE

EQUATING RESOLVE

*- Surface Heat-*

# The Last Poem

### 1.

I held her body,
> carried her to the opening.

We spoke of what would become of us,

> the night, a shadow etched in formlessness.

We knew the scent,
> familiar like a long return.

Now, at the end, a reticent
> call to memory –

the earth now retreating, now emerging –

(the temptation to run), the wound cut into
> the very fabric of being.

We waited for reprieve, for the land to return
> scant and ready: destined.

### 2.

If I run,
> don't be alarmed.

I carry on in the desert heat,
> a compromise of belief.

The breath is human.  It wakes me
> from deep sorrow,

breaks and tears with hammer
> and nail.

3.

Time will take us.

The weight of it, also submerged,
carried like a chipped tooth,

a faded tattoo, a sea lion
cresting the rocky shore.

We trade in our bodies,
we transmit useless projection.

All the broken promises,
the pages painted on sand –

a diaspora of self.


4.


Long cast out,

      I've retrieved the line.

## Lioness

You were with the lions.

They were aware of your fire –
how they roared!

I believed the zoo had opened its gates,
and let the monkeys drink from my water bottle.

They tried smoking –
the chimpanzees enjoyed it,

the gorilla didn't agree.

In past the knotweed,
some kid used whiteout to paint

the name *Sean* on the locust.
I threw stones at the tree.

I often stoned the tree.

There was char and ash deep
down in the woods,

and I haven't heard from you in weeks.

Rain came down and drew
snakes from the reptile garden.

I knew then that they had taken you.

The lions were aware of your passing –

you camped down there with Emile for weeks,
but Roe vs. Wade just got overturned,

and keeping the baby was out of the question.

You turned on me that week.
I was sure you'd never come back this time,

and you never did, to my lion tattoo
I had etched on my arm.

You thought you needed a safe place,

that I would do you harm,
but you had your fist in the lion's mouth,

and your voice grew soft.

It was hit or miss, but I looked for your remains.
I never found a skull, a tooth or a brain.

I was knighted that evening beneath
the Royal Shakespeare Company's

lights at the mansion,

where Kate Middleton gave you the credit card
and the use of her gold Mercedes.

I walked home and ate pierogies
and fed the cats,

afraid you would still call the cops
if I didn't keep them fat.

I bought food from Chewy every week
just to keep them off my back.

Every night I walked over to the convent
and brought the rest of your belongings.

I walked there with my slippers on,
the ones we got the time we went

to the Dollar Store, and you were happy
they had the Smarties you were always looking for.

I thought Sr. Rose knew you were there.
She was always so happy to see me.

Right before the rookie cop walked up my stairs,
I wrote the last two checks I would ever write

for the apartment.

You kept telling me that that guy sold the house
and you were moving out to somewhere safe,

but you put the python around
your waist, and the rain fell that day.

The thunder broke the ceiling
and lightning ruptured

the transformer at the end of Wellesley.
That old bat downstairs kept her lights on dim,

as the energy sucked out of the grid,

and I wondered how she would use her hot plate
to warm up her corned beef and hash.

The cops had really shiny black handcuffs,
and they let me put out my hands out in front

of me, as I didn't have any visible
weapons, only my empty hands.

I guess they were looking for me since 3,
because the hairdresser sent me a Facebook message

I finally read 4 weeks later.

The monkeys started to come over
and climb up back behind the house

and look for shorts in the green ashtray.

They really took to the rolled American Spirits,
but when I started to smoke menthols,

they stopped coming around altogether, like you.

The lions finally got rounded up back
behind the field where your fire left a mark.

Only the cub singed its nose.

I rolled up in a fetal position and cried out
while Nick Cave crooned Skeleton Tree one more time.

It was Wednesday, right before the fourth of July.

For some reason, there weren't any fireworks
that night, I thought maybe there was a terrorist
attack on the Steel Building,

and Bill Peduto took the plunge as the bomb toppled the
building.

He died a hero.

You started to swim the Allegheny right past the dam,
down the Ohio and further south.

I was scared you would drown, but I knew you
were secretly a dryad, and would change form

when you were immersed and would swim to the shore,
covered in seaweed, beer cans and sand,

and change back to human form when the people
would be there with the news crews and cheer you on.

It was a miracle that you swam so hard and fast,
but I knew you, and I've seen it before.

This was when the polar bears started
to come up past the fountain at Point State Park.

You would stop to pet the pale white fur
of the young bears, so far from the Arctic.

Now, the sun beat down and you swam freely
with them and fed them tuna.

The zoo let you keep them –
that was 2 weeks before the lions,

and 3 days before the snakes.

I still couldn't find you,
but last night I turned on Y108

and listened to country songs
until all I could think of was you.

Your dress turned up in the hospital laundry,

and I was sure you tried to meet me there,

but couldn't find me because
they had my birthday wrong.

We have the same birthday,
and the lion tattoo on my left shoulder is still there.

The one I got when we were young.

## Polar Bear

Winter light resonant
with the open transom of sky,

a future designed to break
from the generative ice –

your coat yellowed
by snow:

a heart beat in slow cadence.

## The Warrior's Song

It's the loss of a feather.
It's a broken wing.

It's the disconnect,
the white sand, the loss

of an earring in the fallen leaves,
or a ring caught in a turtle shell.

Soon, she'll bring the brittle bones of birds,
careen and detach and circle the sun.

And, I can't walk. I can't walk up the hill,
the hill next to the lake, closest to the river,

the nameless one that runs
like a serpent along a spine of stone.

The wind falls to caress my fallen form,
where shadows lick at my body's

edges. The sun burns like oil.

My hand reaches for a glass
of water, for the cat's black coat,

like the fractured flame of the breaking
sand – a mirrored pyramid built of basalt.

And, to the victor: victory.
And, to the fallen: no regret.

Cast in iron, the bell rings in another round,
my eyes nearly swollen shut, and I listen

for the sound of vulture wings,
for that coming engine.

# Elysium

The sun has returned, diminished.

We move, battle weary
as the wintering hive –

a resolution to survive,
a whisper of reprieve;

there're rumors of rain.

We see into the fields.

## Solstice of Future's Past

I carry this with me, always.
How we whittle the bone

to a splinter of itself.
How we tend to stone,

mark the tip, fit it to spear.

The day breaks soon
to the sun's darkest

passage, 21 days into
deep December.

The city collapses into
a canopy of arbor.

We hunt under green light,
the street glows in green light,

returns to supernal variations
of surrender –

the causeway, a kingdom of sand.

## Loss

Too narrow to
capture the light –

Greenland swallowed
from an aerial view,

I sought land amid
the concurrent deluge.

I lifted the cover,
the grey stone etching

of your name,
for there is no other,

no link, no cause
from point A to point B.

We hovered over it,
it was the cooling tip

of the combusting engine,
the plane like acne

on the hollow face of youth.
I broke from my silence,

and the whole world split in two.

There was a rendering
of a new sphere, a new planet.

It carried more than memory;

it rained down from heaven
reverence and repair.

## Flight

Beyond the white room,
my words, heavy with snow,

a display of comfort:
these things lead to the heart.

The cats linger
by the heat vent,

and you're curled in blankets
in the heavy shade of winter.

I look at you, and in my mind,
I disarm the multitudes,

shield you from the arrow's strike.

I take you in my arms,
take flight, take wing.

## Bushfire

A koala, carried from the flame –
how she's carried to safety,

how she's carried tenderly
across the scorched earth.

I hear, I respond,
nearly broken –

a chance of immersion
in deepening waters.

Every day, I relearn the measures
of survival, to let go,

to recognize impermanence.

What do we do now,
when things are changing so rapidly –

the near impossible sense
of how to respond, to tread the water

of fate, to conjure luck within
the energetic body of the planet.

I'll carry these lines with intent.

Faced with impossible odds,
I'll remain courageous,

carry water from outstretched hands.

## Three Sisters

I shy away from time,
and it in turn devours me.

See how the hawk
takes the pigeon?

We're speaking
of certain rhythms

in the consequence
of time, but it's only

a piece of glass on
the sidewalk,

a shredded straw
in the door of the tunnel.

We speak of things
delivered:  a particle,

a piece of the whole.

I know there's little
to contend with,

we're between reason
and the slow cadence

of the Ohio, her sisters
bleeding into her,

resting on the shoulders
of iron.

A grip of thunder in storm clouds:
a pulse, a response –

a lift to the arching causeway,
a trio of horns, heralding flight.

## Collecting Skulls

When I reveal this,
                I decompose
and the body migrates
          to grey flesh, ash,
                    isolated,

like a wave of rock
                to strike the skull.

Skulls from stage
              to street:
the terrible leveling of ground.

Skulls in clouds,
                skulls sewn to cloth,
        skulls of birth,
                    skulls of death,
skulls of snow-blinded breath.

Skulls of steel,
                skulls of spirit;

how the richness of my bones
                build upon bones – a mosaic,

a white-washed history of skulls,

        the eyes blackened, and tied to the ways
skulls sound in the drumming ground –

(little worms, wind chimes),

bird skulls, an errant hare, down in the dirt,

down in the company of skulls.

# Reincarnation

The skull is blessed –
what remains, a reflection

of the mutable eye.

A flower for each crevice,
the brow crowned in flowers,

the snow lily protrudes.

And when she comes home,
she is a kingfisher on

the Shannon. She moves
in rhythm with the river,

exits the water, consumes
death's sway.

Bones sing to the horn,
the clang of the gong.

Shadowy wings
advance and retreat,

still palpable, alive
in cold memory.

## Empty Hand

Not always the rage
of a caged tiger –

it can be relieved
of its confines.

At the end of a fist;
a palm, a flower.

Deliver the blow,
return the fist,

blanket the body.

The body, sheer silk
smooth in transition.

These are not flesh and bone;
these are cadence of breath –

a call to resolute posture.

# The Taxidermist

I was surprised that she came over
after the package of ammunition

from Amazon arrived at our house.

I guess you taught her to shoot the Glock
after you met her at the magic mushroom

ceremony out near Bedford.

You started to get a little nervous,
and the dog was dying of cancer.

You said you were going
to do some taxidermy soon,

that his body would always
be enshrined, but you kept the head

and posted it on a stake in front of your house.
She learned to shoot by putting him down.

I thought that she got you
out of the hospital and took you

to your house and gave you a bath.
I haven't seen or heard

from anyone in weeks,
and was starting to fray at the edges.

I couldn't tell if she was gone for good,
but now I knew.

She kept bringing up that guy
who changed the locks on my old house,

but he was long gone and if I saw him again,
I'd punch him in the throat.

I wanted her to know that things
weren't like that anymore,

that things weren't like they were before,

but both of you didn't answer any of my calls;
both of you tried to forget me.

It was hard to go to *Tea Bags* and not be able to smoke.

Goat spent a lot of money on gin and tonics,
and you brought the dog head in a sack

and dropped it on the bar to protest the no smoking.
I had a beer with you and we lit up until

the bartender told us they would call the cops
if we didn't put out our smokes.

It was rare for me to drink –

it's been awhile.

She got the note I sent her and still she didn't respond.
I saw that guy in the corner

and punched him in the throat.
I threw away his cane.

The cops came again and dragged me off.
She just looked at me.

You attached the head to the dog's body,
and sewed up the remains.

*-Gathered Triune-*

# Flies

There are more good days
than bad days, now.

I am looking for something
to sustain us.

The lamp light is warm,
dishes are done.

I am older in the guise
of the young.

I speak in strange tongues,

still, the pheasant looks out
of place where it resides.

Maybe it's the snow that holds
its feathers close to the ground.

This makes a difference.

I would like to attract flies to this jar.
I wrap it in fly paper, inside the glass.

We'll put this into motion,
keep them steady on trapped air.

# Wake

the wake is over
now we tend to the living
rain on the sidewalk

# Apology

I'm sorry for the turn of the wheel,
for losing the lead –

my broken stride, a tremble on the ground.

It was a mask,
etched in wood, painted so pristine –

it meant so much to me.

I'm running toward you,
my lines memorized,

my words measured
on the empty page.

(*heart beating, drifting, repeating*)

When I returned from the mountain,
the wolf had eaten from my hand.

Its warm coat kept me warm in bitter night.

My skin, pale in the morning sun,
thawed now, warmed now.

I saw you again,
a heart so golden the light bore through me.

A recognition of self –

(calm removal)

returned.

## Valentine's Day

There's a glimmer at
the back of the room.

It moves through the window glass,
and winks out of sight.

I am drawn to its light,
like sun returning to our doorsteps:

*spread ashes until you are saved*
*by spirit and chance alone.*

Chances are you'll never
know me.

I've made valentines

for the wintering rabbits,
and the feral cats that ride balloons

over the fences, over there, up the hill
                    to god knows where.

## Moon Phase

When I think of your body,
It's not the body

I see when I turn my face,

the cast of light from a shaken
terrace, the glint

of lamplight in broken pairings.

When I think of your body,
it's not the body I feel

when we knew the water
overflowed past the moorings

of the well.

## The Cure for Cancer

Did anyone ever see the smokes
from Korea in the red pack?

They're called *This*, and taste like poison.

I think they might actually be from N Korea,
where Kim Jong-un formulated an alien

cigarette brand with Leonard Nimoy

that had the capacity to cure cancer
if smoked in small amounts.

Last summer, there were so many alien
spacecraft in the night sky,

that I knew I was from another galaxy,
and quietly waited for my transport.

The way to my solar system was a portal
through the sun, and my Mom and Dad

could actually change form and show
me the way we really looked.

We looked like a shadow of a sunflower
with light pouring out of our darkened edges.

They could also turn into octopi,
as this was what we looked like before

we were reincarnated into humans,
although we weren't really human,

we were inky black sunflower

creatures with light pouring out of us.
I smoked a little bit of *This* tobacco

rolled into a Top cigarette paper,
and had to lay down immediately.

I heard Spock's and Bones' voices
in my head telling me not to drink

any water, as it would exacerbate
the flow of *This* to my bloodstream.

The poison moved slow, and I thought
it was also in the cat food, as N Korea

took over Rite Aid and started to poison cats
with the *This* approach to cancer treatment.

The cat breathed hard on my chest for a while,
but seemed to come through okay.

I got out of bed 30 minutes later,
and I realized the poison had created

a black, viscous layer beneath my skin
like the alien that took Spider-Man, or Venom.

It was something right out of the comic books.

I thought by now packs of *This* were flying
off the shelves, and that people everywhere

knew the secret that N Korea
had infiltrated the tobacco industry.

All it took to cure cancer was a couple puffs of *This*.

## Cinder Blocks

The land is sparse, relocated
by the empty sky.

I lie there with the yellow-
tailed finch – the ones

that move about the sunflowers,
the ones that make me

forget the altered breath
of cages, the summary

of our lives, the initial
grasp of freedom.

We carry cinder blocks across
the yard to the patio,

past the green garage,
and there is a scattering

of alley cats to other parts
of the neighborhood. They become

different hunters.  Then, a *chit chit*
from a squirrel, the loaded resin

of black walnut – the wild hunt
for food stores, the brave search

for survival.

## A Long Overdue Response

Draw from me
the web of existence,

breathe in and out:
a sunrise in the blink of an eye.

Relinquish from your pockets –
                a button, a bit of thread,
cold money, candy twisted in foil.

I sing of your light –
                the flutter of the nuthatch,
shaded from a dim future.

There's hope in the lit corner.

It begins to fade in the thunderous echo
of intent. We're brothers, see?

They can't rip out our hearts like we do.
They only see what they want to see,

make of us what they want to,
call us what names they will.

Tread softly on grey concrete,
                in fields of lavender
these bars hold us close.

I will be your footprints.

I will be your breath.

Here, I find solace in the carrying forth.

## Butterfly

You say, you can't keep
the world from collapsing

when it has already collapsed.

A thin thread holds us –

tongue protrusion,
keeper of the butterfly.

I ask you,
*breathe life into me.*

Release me from the wreckage.

Keep me close to you,
collected and pinned.

What will remain
after rain clouds, then rain?

Beneath it, I call upon an olive branch.

# Wood Street Station

The last sun-lit hour,
in between the last

bus from downtown,

I hear sirens wail like fences
covered by dirt, looking to

the city that burns against
the remaining light.

I build from beneath, the architect
of new dreams – sprouted grass

from the concrete, the pigeons
gather and flock to the sound

of the bass drone and click.
The music directs me.

I've no way to act other than
to pick words, to pace myself,

to take care in doing so. It seems
like a life and death situation,

to make the right belief pattern,
to coax out meaning.

## Bass Variant

It's unbelievable tension,
metric: unstable in its

variants of color,

a blue sapphire glows
as the light seeping

from a bedroom window.

I'm shepherd of the covenant,
builder of the bonfire,

whisperer of prayer –
a sheepdog otherwise unaware.

Next door, repetition pulses
from the walls;

a bass drum repeats,
*boom, boom ... boom.*

It says, sleep now, tomorrow.

# Firefly

In the picture, your hawkish nose –

my brow caught in an angle
that mirrors your own.

I hold you close to me.

We talk and carry on,
my arms around you,

and I see your hair trained
over your eyes.

You shift in when you talk to me,
find comfort in the jokes

that ease out of us –
a firefly I catch and release.

We've forged a blade
that severs fear.

It falls, as the leaf;
past our body,

cast in light.

*~Equating Resolve~*

## At the Corner of Penn Avenue and the Super Volcano

A volcano coalesces
into a dismissal of thought.

Consider the source, godless
and at her whim,

I do.

I also descend onto
Penn Ave at that same

stop light, the one of car
emissions, turning lights.

There is also sunlight
that I revel in.

And the story of beginnings,
returns to beginnings.

A torn page of an errant bible,
a lock of hair from a plastic

doll. It rests there, a pigeon
perched on the railing.

It hangs from the cross wires

The buildings are torn
to the ground, like sand,

like erupted potholes.

I walk slowly past,
wonder at how they

turn out the slag.

## Dream Turtle

Once, I saw you running.

It was a dream, after
the landslide that moved the trees.

You remain buried back there,
remnants of fur and bone beneath

the forsythia and silver maple.
We suffered the same fate.

We drove in our stakes,
and left what was ours,

only quietly we always knew that
it wasn't, that nothing really is.

We carried what we could.

We moved like the turtle –
the weight of home on our backs.

## Song of Youth

Music, cerebral –
then, from head to heart:

faded fatigues I've carried
since I was 11,

close to my hips now.

I left because I could.

Tenuous, the break at the wrist,
my arm driven into sand,

passed on to scavengers.

Home, like memory,
faded from view.

I place it in prayer,
carry it high atop a plateau –

a subterranean fire.

## Rose

I reach over, touch
its brittle stem.
The dried flower,
preserved, a body
of beauty, a single
gesture to the
stranger sitting beside.
And, there are times
when I can't seem to
find the words.
I think of this rose,
this tiny relation,
cradled by the lamp's
edge, see its sameness,
its resonance
with the brittle quiet.

# When You Turned 79

I remember the green Chevelle –
the sun was shining through the windows.

You just picked me up from preschool.
It was noon, and your hair was long.

You looked at me and smiled,
we were going home.

Life was slow and just forming.

When I got to my room,
there was a Star Wars action figure on my pillow –

a gift for the end of my first year of school.

I think it was Luke Skywalker
in Bespin fatigues.

That was right before Han
said goodbye to Chewie,

and was taken by the carbon freeze.
Now, you're producing hip-hop records,

and Snoop Dog is a regular at your house.

Dad turned the whole front yard
into a pasture for goats.

He bought a red tractor, and plowed
Barbara's field under.

He was living his dream of being
a farmer, and bought a lease

for the land to cultivate hemp.

I was stuck at my apartment,
but I kept hearing the new

Snoop Dog song on WAMO.

I couldn't really believe how far you'd come
with your tech skills –

the whole basement was converted
into a state-of-the-art studio.

I couldn't help it, it was your birthday,
and my cell phone had a N Korean virus

on it that was making it hard to call.

The whole screen popped up
as a nuclear missile launching site,

with little squares all over the screen.

Every time I tried to call you,
it would open like a hatch over

a missile silo.

The bomb was hanging over Pittsburgh,
waiting for me to deliver.

I freaked out and turned the phone
completely off. I threw it in the weeds.

That was the second time I lost my phone that week.

There was nuclear static all through the air;
a red web-like static that kept my eyes shut

and kept my eyes sizzling.

You aren't so young anymore,
but your music production company

just brought in 2.5 million.

I was in the woods, deep in,
talking to monkeys in a deserted neighborhood.

I guess everyone evacuated
because nuclear war was being waged –

the orange alert: the deep summer
heat swallowing me whole.

# Revolution

The decay of freedom,
the ancestral divide

from word to page,
shaken from the foundation

like a curse of ants
to the gaping mouth:

the splintered wood
of a door worth shutting.

There are armies built
for such things,

as there are revolutionaries
that act as your neighbors,

to confide in and resist us.

Still, the ox cuts through grass,
the hand that feeds recoils,

and the elevated rate of change
plunders us.

There is a startling moment,

a frequent bearing of destiny
that deserts us,

and you are directed
to a new possibility,

to wake from chrysalis.

## Now, Arriving

I walk into the looming
present, without a trace

of past or future.

The remedy is a simple
mixture of water and salt –

the ocean in motion;

each morning, the sun.
I look out over the houses,

at the trees that hover
over the rooftops.

How the limbs dangle
and drift in and out.

Without the deep earth,
the wind would topple them.

I look at my hands,
measure the creases in my fingers,

release the treasure I find,
beautiful and transparent;

relinquished to this moment.

## Hearing Klee

Trying to comprehend
metallic birds –

canvas of sound,
blanket of white.

Mechanical brush;
air under my feet,

flutist pauses.

## Milkweed

Stand with me,
carry me.

Love me,
care for me.

Hands like a flower
in deep summer.

The feathered resonance
of milkweed

in deep summer.

The days continue
because of you,

your ability to endure
through loss.

Close knit, you carry
on like a butterfly –

resilient now,
how you carry on

transformed.

## New City

Is it lost ancestry?
A gap in the celestial columns

where we once walked?

The evidence is vital
to the blasted rock.

We tar ourselves to wood,
create something out of fire.

There are tendencies of forgiveness,
centers of navigation,

revolutions of time, tires burning
through the corroded streets.

I walked to the outskirts of the city,
saw the pummeled fountain against

the skyline. I knew a tender
wind from the water.

Lights shifted as a river barge
carried its burden.

I saw the living endure

## Early May

When we'd drive
past the cemetery

on early mornings,
the sun burning

through the clouds,
the weeping willow

greening in the avails
of May.

It was every spring,
every turning leaf

so jubilantly aware.

## Key

Walk with me.

We have arrived.

The red-headed
woodpecker still

against the bark.

There is a time
to close the door

on reflection,

and begin to practice
what we've seen.

There is a way to reach
beyond the towering bridge

and build from beneath.

Here we are. We've found
the door and turned the key.

# Storms of July

1. Projection

The black oak yields –
a window of heat

in radiant light.

It stands not because of you,

but beneath the canopy
where the dogs are set loose.

I ash in the dust,
lay the branches close

until wind or rain carries them.

> *Bring water*

> *Clear the way*

> *Fill the roots*

> *Nourish the leaves*

I rub the ash into dust,
feel the heat leave the moss

beneath me, and carry the long rain.

2.   Journey

A hawk cries out, carries on,
cries out again.

Enter the mockingbird,
as the storm moves in.

It orchestrates its noise:

a thunder hammer, goat hooves,
lightning.

You're away –
an abandoned train car to shelter in

(to have refuge, to seek haven).

3.  Return


The raven has returned
to the neighboring ash –

limbs left to ground
like Bragi's tongue.

Turns of summer
in 4am summer rains,

and I'm listening to you sing
in the kitchen –

azure skirt, combed back hair.

I lean over, lift the window.
The leaves reflect:

translucent green.

## Gavel Strikes

Sitting here, I realize;

*empty vessel*

close to the concrete stair,
watching the moon rise.

August wanes like no other.

Heat leaves the sky,
passes on to the hemisphere.

We adapt to change,
move as the gavel strikes

to bleed its thin parchment.

# Home

I walked home today, and felt
the cold stir the air –

the oncoming turn of seasons.

I woke from my rest last night,
and spoke into your ear.

I said things that made you laugh,
and it lightened my heart.

This forms us, now. Like the clay
that circles the potter's wheel.

We're formed by invisible hands.

We're pushed into the clouds that lift
our heels and propel us past

gravity. We reach for refuge,
past the hordes and their crawling.

## Coda

*Reach me,*
*look into me.*

*So small,*
*hands reaching into space.*

*The curve of the moon,*
*retreating to earth's face.*

*Reach me,*
*look into me.*

*So small,*
*hands reaching into space.*

*The curve of the moon,*
*retreating to earth's face.*

Kevin Finn is a poet, musician, visual artist, and martial artist. He is the author of *Exit Wounds* (Amsterdam Press) and *Sea of Dust* (Six Gallery Press). He lives in Pittsburgh, PA.

Acknowledgements: "Collecting Skulls" was previously published in *Death Hums*. "The Warrior's Song" was previously published in *North American Review*. "Early May," "Key," and "Butterfly" were previously published by *SNHL Poem a Day*.

www.ingramcontent.com/pod-product-compliance
Lightning Source LLC
Chambersburg PA
CBHW061317120626
46546CB00007B/2629